Hiding

In

Plain Sight

Discovering Life's Unearthed Treasures

Charmas B. Lee

Author's Note

Some people say there are few things in life of which you can be certain. You will live, die, and of course, you **will** pay taxes.

If that really is the case, I am a very fortunate man. In my life, there is something much more certain. Every second of every minute, every minute of every hour, every hour of every day, while I am awake (and sometimes even when I sleep) I cannot wait to create a positive change in someone else's life. Helping others recognize their value is what motivates me. Love will not let me wait. I have learned that the world is filled with beauty when the heart is full of love.

The journey that I am going to share with you will be very personal and intimate in nature. Each story is a retelling of true events. The trials that we encounter introduce us to our strengths. Life is a continuous process of education, the world is the classroom, and those with whom we come into contact are our teachers. We are never too young to teach and never too old to learn.

If you are not grounded in truth, the ebb and flow of life can toss you around like an unmanned ship on the sea of tribulation. We are always on the precipice of greatness; however, for many of us with victory in sight, we settle for mediocrity.

Life is a treasure hunt. There is inspiration everywhere. By taking this walk with me, I hope that you will have a new view—perhaps even a fresh perspective on life. Life's true beauty lies in the **mind** of the beholder.

"Gratitude and resentment cannot coexist."
Henri J.M. Nouwen

CONTENTS

Introduction 1

Chapter 1: Faith 5
Chapter 2: Discipline 19
Chapter 3: Courage 39
Chapter 4: Commitment 47
Chapter 5: Inspiration 59
Chapter 6: Victory 69
Chapter 7: Leadership 79
Chapter 8: Love 89

My Lifetime Value 97

Appendix 101

About the Author 103

Cole
It was an honor to be your coach
Be blessed
Chris Z

ACKNOWLEDGEMENTS

I want to extend my personal and sincere thanks to every individual mentioned in this book. You have changed my life forever. I would also like to applaud Shannon Steward, Sherry and Al Alvares, Joe Aldaz, Teresa Kolar and Jeff Huisingh for the behind the scenes support of this endeavor. Last but not least I'd like to thank Janice, the positive motivating force within my life.

INTRODUCTION

As I walked the parade field at the United States Air Force Academy Preparatory School, I knew that I was not myself. I had no joy. My zeal for life was gone. What I was feeling was beyond pain. I was surely at the end of my rope. It appeared that my life had been a series of premature mishaps. The past couple of years were the most difficult that I had ever experienced. My low point was when my home was a 1988 Jeep Cherokee.

The period from January 1998 through November 2001 will forever serve as a blue print in my mind. In January 1998, my youngest daughter was born. The joy and excitement I felt were short lived. She was born premature, weighing 2 pounds, 9 ounces; she also came into the world with a birth defect called EATEF. It was devastating. My bundle of joy lived in the NICU for 6 months. It was touch and go the entire time. Seven months later, my oldest son Deondre passed away. Deondre was a cool, fun-loving kid. He was born with sickle cell anemia. In August 1998, the disease got the best of him and he passed on. The stress and sorrow in the house became unbearable, eventually resulting in a less-than-friendly divorce. Life became very difficult; the cumulative effect of all the blows sustained over the previous couple of years began to take its toll.

Just when I thought things could not get any worse, my employment was terminated. The Air Force Academy made a unilateral decision to no longer continue the contracts at the United States Air Force Academy Fitness and Sports Center, where I worked as a Health and Fitness Specialist. I really loved that job. My occupation afforded me the luxury of creating positive changes in other's lives. I lived for that opportunity. My job was a labor of love. I typically woke up around 4 a.m. each morning knowing that for the next 12 hours, every second of every minute of every hour I would literally have an opportunity to encourage, coach, and heal.

Well, none of that mattered anymore. I was having a JOB experience; he was the guy in the Bible who lost it all. I had read the story many times, and my heart was stirred. But now that I was living it; my heart was broken. I was coping with the premature birth of my daughter, the premature death of my son, the premature loss of a marriage, and now the loss of my job. Surely a man cannot be expected to survive such direct hits. I was broken. As I crawled out of my car-home that morning, I truly did not expect to see another day. I was in a funk, perhaps even a state of sorrow that left me absent. Defeated by life, I began to seriously consider an exit strategy.

As I walked the parade field that morning, I performed a blameless, selfless inventory and came to terms with where I was in my life: I was a 42-year-old-man who had lost his sense of self—a failure at least by the world's terms. Unimportant and worthless, soon I would not even have a job.

As I contemplated my exit strategy, a car pulled into the parking lot. This is where my life story changed.

CHAPTER 1: FAITH

THE AMBASSADOR

THE AMBASSADOR

Once, or if perhaps you are lucky, twice in a lifetime, someone comes into your life and changes you forever. The effects of those changes are felt at a visceral level. As a result, you reach a higher level of consciousness. You are catapulted to a higher level of self-awareness, developing a new blueprint for living, coaching, working, and believing.

The first time I had this experience was when I met my wife Janice, who I will discuss in a later chapter. The second time was when I trained and coached an incredible athlete named David Mueller, or "Pre," as I referred to him.

Early one Sunday morning, my wife and I were enjoying a beautiful summer day. We had made our normal trip to our local Starbucks, and enjoyed our favorite drinks. The summer was going well. I was blessed with an opportunity to work with one of my former athletes who was drafted by the Cleveland Browns in 2007. In the fall of 2008, he suffered an injury and was back on the mend. He had lost a step and needed to improve his speed. That following summer he came to visit me and asked for my help. He believed that I was the best person for the job, and of course I was thrilled.

Because of his athletic prowess, I needed another athlete who could keep pace with a professional wide receiver. Training the linear expression of speed can be very complicated. Drills to improve nervous system function, running mechanics, and the proper type of strength training were essential to his overall development. The NFL deals in results. Wide receivers come with many attributes and skill sets. However, aside from the ability to catch the ball; speed, acceleration, and first-step quickness are at the top of the list. To accomplish the desired outcome, I needed a battle-tested warrior who possessed these same abilities required to run stride-for-stride with this mammoth of a man. This individual also needed to possess strong mental fortitude, which is typically the biggest obstacle for an athlete as it relates to establishing, maintaining, and increasing the tempo of a world-class training session. In my professional opinion, there was only one person for the job: David Mueller.

Pre was an amazing athlete. I had worked with him for multiple seasons during his high school career. He was a coach's dream. He was coachable, centered, and mentally and physically tough. He had an amazing work ethic, possessed a positive attitude, and never boasted or complained. In fact, he never said much unless you mentioned Stevie Ray Vaughn, one of his favorite musicians. Pre truly demonstrated all the attributes of a champion. He also practiced good nutrition. His body was his temple. He did not drink or do drugs. In fact, Pre did not eat fried foods or refined sugars. He was serious about his health.

Pre was very powerful. I recall that in one of our private training sessions, Pre was performing box hops to a 44-inch platform. He could power up or out like no other athlete I had ever worked with. He was incredibly fast.

Mohammed Ali, former heavyweight world champion, and arguably one of the greatest ever, once boasted; "I am fast, I mean lightning fast. In fact, I am so fast that once I cut off the lights, I jumped in my bed before the room got dark. Man let me tell you, I'm fast!" Mohammed Ali may have been exaggerating about his lightning speed, but Pre was certainly that kind of fast.

I believe that Pre's best race was the 200 meter dash. Watching Pre exit the starting blocks was an incredible sight. From the stands, I gave him **our** favorite cue: push, push, push. So for approximately 22 meters, Pre applied more ground force than any other athlete with whom I had previously worked. During Pre's freshman year at the University of Colorado at Colorado Springs he had broken the previous records in the short sprints.

When I view Pre from the spiritual perspective, as it relates to human performance, there are three amazing men who come to mind. They were all Hall of Famers, so to speak. They were Samson, Solomon, and David. Pre had the power of Sampson, the strongest man ever recorded in scripture; the wisdom of Solomon, the wisest and wealthiest; and the tenacity, competitiveness, and strategic mindset of David, who was known as a warrior, leader, and ultimately the apple of God's eye.

After my wife and I made the drive back home from Starbucks, we went about our normal routine. When I went to check my voicemails, I heard the voice of Pre's mom.

"Charmas, this is Sandy," she said while sobbing uncontrollably, "Pre is dead!"

Surely this could not be true! I had just worked with him the previous Wednesday morning. I played the message again, and to my utter disbelief, it was exactly what I had heard the first time. Pre is dead. I motioned for my wife to listen to the message, and she confirmed what I had chosen not to believe. I did not know how to respond to this information, so I cried, screamed, and fell to my knees. The pain was visceral, and I became sick.

Finally, after several moments, I came to my senses and called Sandy. Daniel, one of Pre's brothers answered the phone. He confirmed that Pre was in fact dead and expressed his and his family's shock. Without hesitation, I asked if I should come over. He said that his mother would indeed appreciate it.

We made the trip across town to Pre's home. This was the longest 25 minutes of my life. While driving, my eyes kept filling up with tears. Each time I attempted to dry my eyes, the waterfall of tears would return. I had to drive slower than usual.

When we arrived at Pre's house, we noticed there were several cars. We knocked on the front door, Daniel answered. We embraced and moved to the living area. The house was quiet. Daniel and Pre's other brother

Adam were there with their own families, and Sandy was there with a few others. As I approached Sandy, the reality of what had occurred began to sink in. As long as I have known Sandy, she always had a smile on her face. She was full of life, had a positive energy, and was always ready to pitch in. At that point in time the details of Pre's death were still unclear.

Sandy approached me and said hello. Initially, I did not reply. As a coach, I have never been absent of words, but that day was different. There were no words; there was only pain and disbelief. Instead, I gave her a hug, hoping that my actions would speak louder than the words that were lodged in my heart.

Over the next couple of days, the investigation into Pre's death revealed that he had been killed as a result of a drunken driving accident. Ironically, the driver of the car was Pre's new roommate. My friend, David Mueller... Pre, was gone. It was very difficult to grasp the gravity of the situation. None of it made sense, at least not in the physical realm.

A short time later, Sandy asked me if I would be willing to give the eulogy at Pre's memorial service which was scheduled for Saturday, July 26, 2009. I was honored, but had not yet come to terms with his death.

I was scheduled to attend the 2009 USATF Level 2 Endurance School in Boulder, Colorado which was scheduled from July 21 through July 27, 2009. Needless to say, my mind and heart were not really into attending the school. With all that had happened, I was distracted. I have to give thanks to my wife during this time. She was wonderful. In fact, instead of attending the coaching education on my own, my beautiful wife Janice and our dog Epic traveled to Boulder for the training. It was nice to have someone to come home to after each grueling day of learning.

The facilitators of the Level 2 clinic were aware of Pre's death. The track community is wonderful and very integrated, and we share each other's burdens. Typically, the first couple of days of the clinic are held in a classroom, and focus on the latest information in sports psychology, exercise physiology, and biomechanics. The last couple of days are held in your event specific selection with 50–60 others from all over the country. There are college-, high school-, and in some cases, even middle school-level coaches. Saturday is test day, and if you pass, you are awarded a certificate on Sunday. When I met my instructors, I asked if I could take the test on Friday evening, explaining that I needed to be back in Colorado Springs on Saturday to give the eulogy at Pre's end of life celebration. They understood and agreed.

I was very fortunate to have two coaches from Colorado Springs, for whom I had a great deal of respect, at this clinic. Max Oliver, the cross country and track and field coach at Pine Creek High School, and David Harmer, the assistant cross country coach at the University of Colorado at Colorado Springs. I felt at home. I struggled throughout the week with various emotions, making it very difficult to focus. My thoughts were all over the place. What would I say at the eulogy? How would I keep it together? The biggest challenge of all was trying to make sense of everything and understand why it was so painful. I had buried my oldest son the summer of 1998. I had dealt with that as well as many other issues over the past 20 years of parenting and coaching. I thought I was battled-tested! But to be honest, this was different.

Friday came before I knew it, and it was time for me to test. My friend David Harmer was also heading back early to attend Pre's memorial service, and also tested early. David just completed his Master of Science degree in exercise physiology, so most of the information on which we were being tested was pretty fresh in his mind David was a God-send. He helped me in the areas in which I was struggling. My mind kept drifting, and like a good coach, he brought me back into a narrow focus. I took the test and I passed it. It was now time for the journey back to Colorado Springs, where, in my mind, I envisioned a much bigger challenge.

It was time to come to terms with my emotions. It was Friday evening and we started traveling south on I-25. Traffic was heavy, so I said a silent prayer and began the 90-minute drive back to our home. For whatever reason, the drive began to soothe my heart. The landscape, mountains, hills, and grass were illuminating. My heart began to dance. I heard the inaudible voice of God. I know it sounds odd, but he began to speak to me—not through my ears, but directly into my soul. My heart was the recipient of an unexpected gift. My higher power had cared enough about me to share an absolute truth in a way that I could understand it. I turned to my wife and communicated what the spirit had told me. She smiled. Like I said earlier, she is a very special person. She is truly God's gift to me. She understands my spirituality and does a great job of helping me navigate this life. I went home and put the words to paper that were spoken to my heart about David. I titled it, "The Ambassador." I have included an excerpt from that message which follows.

"David was an ambassador of goodwill, sent to this earth in life's form to teach us how to love one another. David was humble, kind, generous and never boastful. It is very unfortunate that David, Pre, has left the earth, but

I can also appreciate the fact that David was a modern-day angel who walked the earth and it was simply time for him to go back home. All of us will sincerely miss David, but I guess we have to understand that his work was done and Heaven was missing an angel."

Many positive things have come to pass since David left the earth. DieM Sportsgear was founded in David's name by his family. DieM gives back 30 percent of their profits to various youth sports organizations and individuals who are in need. They also recognize outstanding individuals who demonstrate the hallmarks of Pre. There is also David's Fund, which also recognizes the value of helping others and is equally generous in its support of athletes and teams. Each year, there is a 5K or a celebration in honor of David and his legacy. Like all of the other greats, there will never be another Pre. Pre, until we see you again, keep on running!

Coach Lee

Coaching Points:

- Sometimes our life's purpose is discovered through a painful experience.

- There are angels that walk the earth hiding in plain sight.

- Never cease doing good; it makes the world a better place.

CHAPTER 2: DISCIPLINE

*YOU ARE NEVER TOO OLD TO LEARN,
AND NEVER TOO YOUNG TO TEACH.*

YOU ARE NEVER TOO OLD TO LEARN,
AND NEVER TOO YOUNG TO TEACH.

The first time I met a young athlete named Kita, she was 9 years old. Kita came from a good family. Kita's parents and I became close friends and continue that relationship to this day. Kita was a very good soccer athlete; however, she had come to the Speed Track and Field Program in an effort to get faster for soccer and explore other sports in which she could potentially excel. I worked with Kita for one season in 2002, and I did not see her again until she was 13.

Kita returned to the Speed Track and Field Program the summer of 2006. Kita had decent speed and probably would have been a better-than-average-sprinter. However, there was something about this young athlete's personality and bio-motor abilities (speed, strength, flexibility, and coordination) that indicated her strength may lie in the area of the hurdles. In my many years of coaching, I had discovered that younger female soccer athletes tend to make pretty good hurdlers. Typically, they are fearless, possess an uncanny frequency, and are good at negotiating the 8.5-meter restriction associated with the event. I asked Kita to give it a try, and in a very short period of time, through trial and error, she became pretty good at it.

One of the greatest challenges a coach faces is the constant battle against mediocrity. Sometimes, the efforts to motivate, educate, and inspire athletes to achieve their full potential can become extremely demanding. Coupled with life's distractions and other outside influences, coaching can sometimes become overwhelming.

There was a particular day during practice that the team did not bring its typical energy or strong mindset. While performing their neuromuscular integration drills, they seemed to be going through the motions. The workout and their work ethic were both less than mediocre. It was impossible to get the student athletes to focus. Focus was a significant part of the mental mastery associated with our practices. My attempts to forge a link between attention and excellence were not working.

Finally, out of frustration, I stopped the practice and motioned to the athletes to move towards the bleachers, have a seat and collect their thoughts. In my then

18 years of coaching, I had seen this behavior many times. Good had become the enemy of great. After all, we were winning and man-handling our competition. We had become complacent, and the athletes did not realize this was a precursor to disaster. I was looking for a champion—someone who was like-minded and driven to win. I was looking for an athlete who would lead by example with a voice other than my own, to direct the team. As a coach, I was driven by excellence.

I knew that if excellence was the standard, then greatness in every aspect of the word must be the goal.

It was then that I was reminded of a quote from Vince Lombardi, legendary former NFL coach of the Green Bay Packers.

"We will relentlessly pursue perfection, knowing full well we won't catch it. Nonetheless, we are going to chase it, because in the process we will catch excellence. I am not remotely interested in being just good."

Armed with this thought, I knew it was time to confront the problem.

As the athletes were sitting in the stands, I called them up one by one and asked them a very simple question: I asked them what I was thinking. Each athlete had a different response, but none of them had the response I was looking for.

When it was Kita's turn, she replied, "You are thinking that I am going to win."

When I asked her how she knew that, she responded with, "Because that is what I am thinking!"

I was ecstatic with Kita's response for many reasons. For one, she had called me Coach Charmas. I had never had an athlete address me that way. It was a form of respect that I had never experienced. It was always either Coach Lee or Mr. Lee. Our culture had popularized young people calling adults by their first names. Some of the children on the team would call their parents by their first names; however, it was not permitted in my camp. To me, it was very disrespectful and suggested an inflated sense of entitlement. In my camp, athletes were not permitted to call coaches by their first or last names.

"You are thinking that I am going to win," was such a profound statement coming from a then 14 year old. It was spoken in a gentle voice, but with an amazing authority. When I asked her how she knew what I was thinking,

I was digging deeper to see if, in fact, she meant what she said. Her response was the validity that I needed. Finally, here was an athlete who was like-minded, driven by excellence, ready to lead by example, and willing to pay the price for success.

On that day, I knew that I had found the champion I sought. Kita was unique and was destined to be great. I pulled out a piece of paper with a quote on it and asked Kita to read it aloud. It was a quote from Epictetus, a Roman teacher and philosopher. Epictetus had been born a slave and was later freed and became a teacher and philosopher. One of his most distinguished students was Marcus Aurelius Antoninus, a leader who through tremendous leadership, strategic planning, and hard-fought battles, established the Roman Empire. Epictetus taught his students the importance of action as a way to personal freedom, to effectively meet the challenges of life, and to reach their full potential.

Kita read the quote aloud.

"Tentative efforts lead to tentative outcomes. Therefore, give yourself fully to your endeavors. Decide to construct your character through excellent actions and determine to pay the price of a worthy goal. The trials you encounter will introduce you to your strengths.

Remain steadfast...and one day, you will build something that endures: something worthy of your potential."

Epictetus, Roman teacher and philosopher 55–135 A.D.

I asked her to memorize the quote and explain its meaning to me. At the following practice, Kita recited the quote with passion and enthusiasm. She explained that it meant to give it your all. I told her from that moment all that I wanted her to give is all she had. Over the next several years, the quote became the team's mantra.

PERSEVERANCE, COURAGE, CHARACTER, AND HUMILITY

It takes a lot of courage and intestinal fortitude to get up and keep on fighting. After a great summer season, Kita qualified for the 2006 USATF Junior Olympic Nationals in Baltimore, Maryland. It was her first national-level competition. Kita's first race was the 200 meter hurdles. Kita ran an amazing race and had a significant lead heading into the fifth and final hurdle. Then, the unthinkable happened.

Kita clipped the hurdle with her lead leg, which is typically a hurdler's nightmare. Fighting desperately to keep her balance, she finally tumbled to the ground. Three of her competitors ran past, exempting Kita from making the finals. Kita was devastated. The fall had left her physically and emotionally bruised. As my wife and I had watched the race from the stands, our hearts sank. It seemed like it took forever for Kita to finally fall. I was thinking, "Stop fighting gravity, fall, get up and finish the race; you will still win your heat and make the final."

In hindsight, I failed to remember that Kita was also a very good soccer player. Negotiating speed, balance, and coordination at high speeds while performing amazing footwork was not foreign to her. Fighting was the natural thing to do! Equally devastated were Kita's mother and grandparents who were also watching from the stands. They were not devastated because of the fall, but rather from the distress of seeing a loved one hurting.

It took Kita a long time to come back to the area where we were sitting. When she did, she spoke with her family. As I watched her interaction with her family I began to study her paraverbals, or body language. I had picked up this skill when I worked at the Colorado School for the Deaf and Blind. Kita's head-down, slumped shoul-dered posture suggested disappointment. However Kita's disappointment was not in herself; instead, it was the type of disappointment one has when he or she lets someone else down. After all, Kita had competed very well. There was nothing else that she could have done. Exhausted, yet not victorious, she left everything on the track. Kita had run a tremendous race against some of the best youth athletes in the United States. Moreover, she had walked away with only a minor ankle injury. Without making any eye contact, she walked to where I was seated.

This was my opportunity to motivate, educate, and inspire Kita with a truth that she had not yet realized. I learned through trial and error that there is a fine line between **constructive** and **destructive** criticism. Coaches possess a tremendous amount of power and influence. Through our communications, we may humiliate, humor, hurt, or heal. My approach is to give **rise** to athletes by shifting their thinking. Athletes are never only as good as their last race. Your lifetime value is not determined by the place in which you cross the finish line. I developed my coaching style by standing on the shoulders of those who, in my opinion, had been or still are humanitarians and great leaders of men. In that moment several of the "great ones" came to mind including Vince Lombardi, Ronald Reagan, Dr. Martin Luther King, Jr., John Wooden, Phil Jackson, and Pat Riley. However the quote that came to mind was spoken eloquently by Teddy Roosevelt in 1910.

"It is not the critic who counts, not the man who points out how the strong man stumbles, or where the doer of deeds could have done them better. The credit belongs to the man in the arena, whose face is marred by dust and sweat and blood, who strives valiantly... who knows the great enthusiasms, the great devotions, who spends himself in a worthy cause, who at the best knows in the end the triumph of high achievements, and who at the worst, if he fails, at least fails while daring greatly, so that his place shall never be with those cold and timid souls who have never known neither victory nor defeat." Teddy Roosevelt "Man in the Arena," April 23, 1910

Armed with Mr. Roosevelt's quote in mind, I stood up and motioned her over and congratulated her on the race.

"Kita, today I saw a glimpse of your potential and wow, you are even greater than I imagined!"

Kita looked puzzled. I gave her a hug and asked her to have a seat. My wife Janice had recorded the race, and I urged Kita to take a look at it. "Kita you are going to be fine. I want you to take a look at this footage so you can see what the crowd and I witnessed—a Champion in the making!"

As my wife showed Kita the footage, another Colorado coach came by and patted Kita on the back. It was Coach Mack. He was a friend and very good jump coach who worked with another club program. I will never forget what Coach Mack said. "Girl you were moving. Great race!" His timing could not have been better. Kita respectfully thanked him. Coach Mack replied, "Kita, pick your head up; you are going to be winning a whole lot of races."

We went through the footage and Kita saw how far ahead of her competitors she was prior to her fall. She also had a chance to hear the crowd's reaction. She began to smile.

Kita had also qualified in the 100 meter hurdles; however, she was not ranked in the top 15. If Kita was going to make the finals, she would have to run a personal best. After a brief discussion on the 100 meter hurdles and the proper treatment for her ankle, Kita and her family went back to their hotel to rest and prepare for the next day's competition. The next day, Kita ran a personal best in the prelims of the 100 meter hurdles, and qualified for the finals, finishing seventh overall in her first national competition!

Kita's high school career was filled with many challenges that she truly turned into opportunities.

FRESHMAN YEAR

As a freshman, Kita developed pneumonia and her training was sporadic. Kita maintained a good attitude and trained through the adversity, setting a new school record and placing second at the Colorado High School State Championships.

SOPHOMORE YEAR

Early in Kita's spring track and field season, she hit a hurdle, striking the ground extremely hard. It was as though when her body met the ground, the earth moved. In an attempt to break the fall, she extended her arm and ended up with a *Galeazzi fracture.

Kita, her parents, my wife and I spent the evening in the emergency room. The Galeazzi break changed the entire dynamic of the season for her. Kita could not train with hurdles, and was not able to perform any weight-bearing activities. It appeared that Kita's season was over. It would have been easy for Kita to quit, and certainly understandable, but she did not. Kita's mental and physical

*The Galeazzi fracture is an injury involving a radial shaft fracture with associated dislocation of the distal radio-ulnar joint. The injury disrupts the forearm axis joint.

fortitude were demonstrated by her willingness to be patient, not give up, and trust in herself, a higher power, and her coach. Kita continued her quest to be the very best.

Choosing the proactive approach, Kita's doctor, parents, and I continued to work within the scope in which we were able. I was a strength coach and health and fitness specialist. More than that, I was a Kita fan! If Kita was willing to do the work and trust her training, I was willing and excited to develop a hurdle-specific strength and conditioning program that was not contraindicative. Kita finished fifth at the Colorado High School State Championships that year, which was quite an accomplishment based on the adversity she had experienced that year.

JUNIOR YEAR

Kita went on to become a two-time USATF National Junior Olympic finalist. She met the qualifying standards for the prestigious Junior USA's in the 400 meter hurdles. That same year, Kita also set records in the 100 meter and 300 meter hurdles at Cheyenne Mountain High School, and was the second leg of the state champion 4x100 meter relay team. It is important for me to mention that through it all, win or lose Kita remained humble, never displaced blame, and always carried herself in a very dignified manner.

SENIOR YEAR

Kita had an incredible senior year. She became a two-event state champion in the 100 meter and the 300 meter hurdles (tying the state record in the 300 meter hurdles). Kita was voted "Prep Athlete of the Year" by the Gazette Telegraph.

Kita is in college now and still excels in both athletics and academics.

Life is a continuous process of education; when the student is ready, the teacher appears. You are never too old to learn, and never too young to teach. I also find spiritual relevance in Isaiah 40:29-31 which states: "He gives strength to the weary and increases the power of the weak. Even youths grow tired and weary, and young men stumble and fall; but those who hope in the Lord will renew their strength. They will soar on wings like eagles; they will run and not grow weary, they will walk and not be faint."

Below is the "Significant Influence" Essay that Kita wrote as part of her college admittance essay.

"All I want is all you've got." These words, spoken by my track coach, Charmas Lee, exemplify what he expects from his athletes he coaches and from himself.

He demands nothing less than your best each time your spikes hit the track. Further, he requires the lessons being taught on the track be applied to your life; set goals about the process of reaching the outcome, be willing to invest your time and energy, stay in the "learning zone", sustain concentration, listen and be receptive to feedback, work diligently on elements needing improvement, take time to restore yourself, become a great performer.

It was the first meet of the track season in 2004 and my first time competing on Coach Lee's team, Speed Track and Field. There I was, a twelve-year-old, drenched with emotions and lacking confidence. For days, I had been crying, worried about this event. I was shaking inside as I warmed-up for my first race, the 200-meter dash. Coach Lee was on the infield giving me reassurance as the dreaded moment crept closer. He told me that "the hay was in the barn" and I was ready to run. As I finished the race, I looked up to see how horribly I had done, but to my surprise, there was not anyone ahead of me. Coach Lee told me to have faith in what I was doing and to believe in myself. Being prepared is imperative but belief in oneself imparts courage. Coach Lee has helped me gain self-confidence and I have learned to believe in myself. Belief in oneself is the highest form of self-respect.

Puke Hill. The name alone is enough to scare away most people. Each season, the Speed Track and Field team takes on this grueling, 40-meter incline. We simply run up the hill repeatedly until we throw up, then we run up it some more. This workout breaks you down physically and mentally. Out of bed at 5:30 a.m., the anticipation of the pain about to be experienced is nerve racking. Even the descent is tough after you just lost the oatmeal you ate for breakfast and your legs feel like jelly. Coach Lee stands at the top yelling out our times and encourages us to press on through the pain. After ten, eleven, twelve hill repeats, I hear, "That was incredible!" A sense of accomplishment sweeps over me. I have done what I did not think I could do, gone further than I thought possible. Puke Hill is where I learned that there is always more inside to give. Coach Lee has challenged me to go beyond what I think is my best effort.

The summer of 2009 brought some devastating news when David Mueller, a fellow Speed Track and Field athlete, was killed in a single car, drunk-driving accident. At practice I saw Coach Lee, who is always so authoritative and strong, break down. He pours his heart and soul into every athlete he trains and David's death was the equivalent of Coach Lee losing one of his own children. I realize what a privilege it is to be one of his athletes and I am motivated to live up to his expectations. My spirit has been infiltrated with his passion and now my standards of excellence are higher, my beliefs are stronger and my dreams are bigger.

I try to assimilate what I learn from Coach Lee and strive to apply these ideals to everything I do. I accept challenges and embrace hard work knowing that success happens over time with deliberate practice. Coach Lee has a special gift that allows him to bring out the best in people and he has, without a doubt, brought out the best in me. One day, I hope to be as great a performer as Coach Lee believes I can be.

Kita's actions spoke much louder than words ever could. She inspired me in many ways. Because of Kita, I am a better person and a better coach. Life has taught me that it is important to acknowledge those, both young and old, who have been influential in my life. Kita, you are one of those people. Thank you for the opportunity. It truly has been an honor to be your coach.

Coach Charmas

Coaching Points:

- One's best may be achieved in both victory and defeat.

- To be a champion requires perseverance, courage, character, and humbleness.

- It is not only what you say, it is what you do. Your actions speak louder than your words.

CHAPTER 3: COURAGE

WHEN FEARS AND DREAMS COLLIDE

WHEN FEARS AND DREAMS COLLIDE

At the 300 meter mark of the 400 meter dash, pain sinks its savage teeth into the legs of the athlete, blows flames down his throat, and taunts him to run faster. His face writhes with pain due to the lactic acid accumulation in his legs. For the 400 meter runner, there are few things more inspiring than the roar of the crowd. The last 100 meters of the 400 is typically when the roar reaches a feverish pitch. It is also the most difficult part of the race. The athlete's position at the end of the race is greatly determined by the effort put in the first three 100 meter legs of the race. It is called race distribution.

As the athlete approaches the back-stretch, the crowd begins to applaud his efforts and the efforts of his competitors. The athlete who was once leading the race recognizes the fact that he is not alone; the wolves are at the door. This is the point in the race where he has to perform a "gut check". For some, it is where their ***fears and dreams collide.***

When fears and dreams collide, the tension of opposites occurs. The tension of opposites is a place in which many of us exist. It is a place where being average has become good enough, but the capacity to achieve more exists.

The tension of opposites creates stress in our lives because being comfortable will never give a voice to our dreams. It makes us aware that our fear of failure is stronger than our desire to succeed. The typically over-exaggerated, anticipated pain, self-doubt, and fear associated with this tension converts necessary efforts of advancement into retreat.

The 400 meter dash is a great metaphor for life; you have to run your race, as designed, based on your ability. There are no medals handed out at the 350 meter mark of the 400 meter dash. To claim your prize, you must finish the race.

Crossing the finish line, he places his hands on his knees, drops his head, and throws up. The race was close. Exiting the track, he takes a quick look at the score board. Nothing yet. Lying down, completely exhausted, he summons up the strength to look up again. Finally, the board lights up. First place!   Exhausted, but victorious.

"Tell me how you did it," I ask.

"Coach," he begins slowly, "At the start of the season you cast a vision and I caught it. You said that it is important to have a world-class vision because during the race you will ask yourself the question what are you suffering for. Losing this race never crossed my mind. My responsibility was to execute my race."

Sometimes you teach what you need to know. For years, I have discussed the importance of vision, preparation, and planning; however; sometimes during the   .
"throes of life," I have forgotten why I suffer.

As I run my own personal 400 meter dash, I am reminded that life requires a 100 percent commitment. The trials that I have encountered have introduced me to my strengths. Absent is the crowd cheering me on at the 300 meter mark. In its place are the memories of those who captured the vision and ran the best race possible on any given day.

There are several instances in which one of my athletes has crossed the finish line, not in first place, exhausted, placing their hands on their knees, and they look up at the score board to validate their efforts. We recognize that one's *personal best may be achieved in both victory and defeat.*

These athletes have taught me how to avoid the tension of opposites. Run the race as designed with prayer, passion, vision, and planning. I have closed the gap between what is deeply important to me and how I spend my time. After all, I will only run one 400 meter dash in my lifetime.

As I celebrate my 101st season of coaching, my hope is that this book will help you run your race. When it is all said and done, you will complete the race, lying on the field victorious. I am eternally grateful for the lessons I have learned from my athletes and others.

Coaching Points:

- There are no medals handed out at the 350 meter mark of the 400 meter dash.

- Run your race, as designed, you are your own competition.

- The trials that you encounter have introduced you to your strengths.

CHAPTER 4: COMMITMENT

I'M GONNA FLY JETS

I'm Gonna Fly Jets

I started coaching Daniel Funk when he was around 13 years old. Daniel had come to the program to improve his speed. He was a very good athlete who played a couple of different sports that required explosiveness, power, and of course, speed. The first day of practice Daniel showed up without his track spikes. Coming to practice without all of the required gear was completely unacceptable. Daniel sat in the stands when he got his first glimpse of "Coach Harmas". Coach Harmas is my self-created alter-ego. He only shows up at times when very firm motivation is required. He is a disciplinarian who speaks at a high volume. My wife calls it my "outside voice". When Coach Harmas surfaces, there is no discussion, no negotiation, and no debate. His communication style is short and firm.

Daniel had the distinct opportunity of meeting Coach Harmas on his first day of practice. Over my years of coaching, I understood that there are only so many times when you can provide honest, constructive, and tempered feedback in this manner. It was important to space these types of communications out during a training season. If a coach was eccentric or nitpicked all the time, athletes would tune him or her out. Making eye contact, I approached Daniel directly and asked him a proverbial million-dollar question. In my years of coaching, not many athletes could address these questions without hesitation or pause.

I asked him what he planned on doing after high school. I assumed this was a pretty demanding and difficult question for an eighth grader. Before I could recite my pre-canned speech that emphasized the importance of preparation, planning, and a quality education, Daniel replied very matter-of-factly, "Coach, I'm gonna fly jets."

Because he had not brought his shoes to practice, it stood to reason that he would not be prepared to respond. Thus, I was not prepared for the answer. However, I was truly encouraged and impressed that this young man had a clue. Daniel's response made me think on my feet. I wanted to make sure Daniel was not simply offering lip service or was being sarcastic.

"Daniel, I am not looking for buddies; I build champions," I began. "Do you plan on packing a parachute when you fly those jets?"

He said that he did.

"Well, in the future think of your shoes and all of the other equipment that you are supposed to have as your parachute. It is better that you have one and not need it, than to need one and not have it," I explained.

Right away, I knew he was going to do well in the program. Daniel was part of the program for several seasons. In fact, he proved to be a very good jumper. He was very coachable; he was a technician and had a strong desire to be successful. That summer, he went on to win the long jump and triple jump at the regional meet in El Paso, Texas. However Daniel did not fare as well at the National Junior Olympics held in Baltimore, Maryland that same summer.

Daniel was very resilient, focused, and hard working. We had a chance to get to know his parents Chris and Tim very well. We felt like members of the family. Daniel also played the violin, and on one occasion my wife and I were invited to watch him at a small high school concert. He and I even had great conversations about life, spirituality, and of course, sports. During his junior year in high school, I gave him the nickname Daniel "Pretty Boy" Funk, since he was a handsome kid the girls loved.

Daniel was consistently persistent. He was never late for practice and performed his warm-up routine with the accuracy of a Rolex watch. He became so proficient that I asked him to become a junior coach, which in our organization was quite an honor. Daniel was recognized as an athlete of distinction, and was the most effective athlete/coach that helped with our Speed Track and Field junior program.

As Daniel went through his high school years, he was faced with many challenges. He had a strong set of values. For a young person, he also had a strong spiritual foundation. From time to time, he and I would discuss some of the challenges that he faced from his peers, we also had some candid conversations about the philosophical differences he had with authority figures. My advice to him was always the same: it was important that he maintained his own identity and did not get caught up in the thick of thin things. Help where you can. Honor God and your parents in all you do. Be an example; keep your property value high through your demonstrations of hard work.

"Daniel," I said, "You are going to change the world."

I recall having a conversation with Daniel and his parents on whether or not he should play football. Like I said earlier, he was quite an athlete; however Daniel seemed to be somewhat susceptible to shin splints and hamstring injuries. He had a disparity in his quad to hamstring ratio. He is what we call "quad heavy" in my profession. Daniel wanted to play, but was concerned about the potential for injury. After our "care conference," Daniel ended up playing football. He had a couple of very good games; however, during one of the games, he was injured. He had a break away, and while running down field, he heard a pop and felt a tear. He was out for the rest of the season and had to have surgery. Post-surgery, Daniel was on crutches and faced extensive physical therapy.

James 1:12 says, "Blessed is the man who perseveres under trial, because when he has stood the test, he will receive the crown of life that God has promised to those who love him."

In spite of his injuries and the ups and downs throughout his athletic journey, he remained upbeat and focused. Daniel later received a proverbial earthly crown by acceptance into the United States Air Force Academy.

He is currently a junior and he continues to excel in everything he pursues.

I know that Daniel's life has a much higher purpose. I believe that the time that he and I spent together only offered me a glimpse of his potential. I believe that wherever he goes, he will become an instant blessing, creating positive change in the lives of many.

The apostle Paul states in first Corinthians 9:26-27 "Therefore I do not run like a man running aimlessly. I do not fight like a man beating the air. No, I beat my body and make it my slave so that after I have preached to others I myself will not be disqualified from the prize."

Daniel's consistent persistence, focus, and discipline remind me of this distinguished apostle.

Daniel's final season with Speed Track and Field ended with an end of season celebration. Daniel's mom Chris shared the essay below titled, "What have we gotten ourselves into?" Needless to say, Mrs. Lee and I were honored.

"What have we gotten ourselves into?"

"Daniel started with Speed T&F in the summer after eighth grade. At our very first practice Daniel got scolded

a bit for not having his cleats with him. And I wondered, **"What have we gotten ourselves into?** *Then came fuel logs, proper fueling, team pushups and puke hill. And I wondered, "What have we gotten ourselves into? "Next thing I knew we were spending longgggg Saturdays in the hot sun in stadiums in Denver. And I wondered,"* **What had we gotten ourselves into***?" Then came a trip to El Paso where we experienced the joy of victory, and a trip to Baltimore where we experienced the agony of defeat. And I wondered,"* **What have we gotten ourselves into?"** *Indoor season rolls around. O dark thirty practices at Monument and downtown, long, sometimes treacherous drives to Boulder on January Saturdays and even longer days in the bleachers. And I wondered,* **"What had we gotten ourselves into?"**

Then I realized we had gotten ourselves involved with a **coach** *who had the knowledge to help our kids be the best track and field athletes they could be. We had gotten ourselves involved with a* **man of God** *who loves our kids almost as much as we do. And who considers it an honor and a responsibility to work with them. We had gotten ourselves involved with a* **mentor** *who helps our kids develop character and work toward lifelong goals. We had gotten ourselves involved with a* **friend** *who was there to celebrate with us in the good times and there to comfort when injuries occurred. (Which was all too* *frequently for us.)We had gotten ourselves involved with a **couple** whose business is a labor of love, who spend countless hours doing for others and who are a blessing to all who have the good fortune of knowing them.*

So I have a little labor of love for you Charmas and Janice. Thank you for being a part of our lives.

Chris Funk

Daniel, your actions speak louder than words. You have inspired me in many ways. It truly has been an honor to be your coach.

Coach Lee

Coaching Points:

- Goals are only wishes until they are written down and practiced daily.

- Consistent persistence is required to accomplish anything of value.

- If you are gonna fly jets, you had better pack a parachute.

CHAPTER 5: INSPIRATION

THE POWER OF A STORY

The Power of a Story

Throughout my coaching career, I have had some very unique experiences. Motivating athletes to become all that they can be is often times very taxing and demanding. I have coached at various levels, but there is nothing that can truly compare to coaching middle school athletes. These children come in all shapes and sizes, and with varying degrees of abilities. For the last 16 years I have coached at North Middle School in Colorado Springs School District 11, the largest school district in the city. Middle school track and field has two distinct seasons in this particular school district. The girls' season typically begins mid-August and finishes the second week in October. The boys' track and field season begins the second week in March and concludes the first week of May. Both seasons end with a district-wide championship called The Classic.

The North Middle School girls' track and field team typically has 80 to 90 participants, ranging in ages from 11 to 14. A typical practice only lasts 45 to 55 minutes. Coaching at this level requires a great deal of planning, patience, and discipline. I truly believe that this is where I realized the importance of forging a link between attention and excellence. Since you cannot afford to waste time, it is imperative to set the tempo and press the agenda, if not, very little will be accomplished. Having the right staff makes all the difference. We have an amazing coaching staff with Gerald Freeman and Arthur Griffin (whom we have nicknamed "Moon") working alongside me. We are known as the three amigos, having grown up together and been great friends for more than 35 years. Mr. Freeman is a teacher's assistant and the head coach. He is great at getting the kids to come out and participate. Coach Moon is the primary jumps coach for the kids.

Back in 2002, North Middle School had a very good eighth grade team. These girls had successfully competed during their sixth and seventh grade years, and by eighth grade, they were now the leaders on the team. We never chose team captains, because we believed that everyone should learn to lead. These young children learned the benefits of personal accountability and had developed great leadership skills at an early age.

From time to time, Coach Freeman held a Saturday practice. It was our way of giving the girls a competitive advantage, as well as a way to ensure they were doing their homework assignments. On a particular Saturday morning, practice was coming to an end and I noticed one of the girls, Alex, sitting on the steps. Something was not quite right. This athlete was typically very up-beat and had a great attitude. On this day, however, she was lethargic and disconnected. I had never ob-served Alex demonstrate this type of behavior before, so I interpreted it as a warning sign. After working with youth and having kids of my own, I know when things are not quite right. I asked Alex how she was doing. She shrugged her shoulders and said that she was doing all right.

"All right," I replied, "It is a beautiful day, the team had a great practice, and we are two weeks away from The Classic!"

Alex explained that her mom had passed away a year prior, and that day was one of those tough days. She was dealing with a silent pain that no young person should have to deal with. Alex continued to open up to me about her mom, and I listened attentively. My heart broke for this brave young girl.

"Alex," I said "I think I know what you are going through. May I share a story with you?"

She agreed. I went on to tell her about my son who had passed. It was easy to tell Alex that Deondre was a wonderful young boy with an incredible spirit. I told her of his number of wonderful qualities and his interest in sports. When I finished, she looked at me in astonishment. I had created common ground with her.

"Alex," I said, "Sometimes I miss my boy very much, and I have learned to keep it all in perspective."

I told Alex that when I am sad, I take a moment to acknowledge how I am feeling and then I remember all the good things about my son. I also believe that one day I will see him again in Heaven. I thanked her for sharing her story with me and I let her know how courageous that was. I told her that she was a champion and that I was proud of her. Her demeanor changed from that of a young person who was defeated to that of someone who had conquered the world. Shortly after that, her dad pulled up and they headed home.

From that day on, Alex seemed to be more determined. She worked hard at practice and ran a better time in the 400 meter dash at the next meet. During our conversation that Saturday, I told Alex that she could accomplish anything she set her mind to. One of her goals was to win the 400 meter dash at The Classic. The day after the second-to-last meet of the season, she came up to me at practice and handed me a note. As I read the note, I was overcome with emotion. I did not realize the importance of the conversation we had that Saturday nor did I understand the impact I had made by sharing my story.

Alex ran well at The Classic, and North Middle School had a tremendous season. Alex's letter to me is below. If you ever have the chance to share your story, do so. The impact may be greater than you could ever expect.

9-26-02

Dear Coach Lee,

I am writing you this letter after the second to last track meet. Something magical happened this afternoon, something wonderful and enchanting. As I was waiting in the line to run the 400M dash, I thought to myself, "Mom, fly with me." Something that I always say to myself before I run, turned into something breathtaking. Usually when I need my mother to be there for me I raise my head and look in the sky and all around me, searching for her, as I raised my eyes to the goal posts on the field I see something miraculous, I see my mother sitting on the goal post, next to her is your son. This has never happened to me before, and at first it scared me. But as I looked harder I saw him smiling so proudly over at you, and my mother at me.

Even though I may be only 13 years old I still know how it feels; the lonely, out of place feeling. But right when I said those words she was there for me. And I know that you son will <u>ALWAYS </u>be there for you. All you have to do is call. He will always hear you, like my mom does.

You have made probably one of the strongest impacts on me than anyone ever has. Not only your strong passion for always helping, but your wise heart. No need to say anything, it's just there. When you told me that you thought I was good enough to do anything I dreamed of, it made my day that much better. And when you told me about your son, I felt that much closer to you. Three years. That's all it takes to give someone that everlasting trust, not only as a track coach, coming then going, but as a person, as a soul.

I know that when you feel upset, I'm not the first person you'll think of, but remember, my mom left me too. To me you are one of the greatest, strongest, loving, and not to mention COOLEST people I have and will ever meet. And I want to thank you from the bottom of my heart for all you have done for me.

I thank you from the bottom of my soul,

Alex

P.S. City, or no city, you will always be the BEST coach ever!

P.P.S. The 400M is mine! I got Rossol in my back pocket! Thank You!

Coaching Points:

- "If your ever gonna see a rainbow, you gotta stand a little rain." - Dolly Parton

- Be an encourager; look long and hard for the opportunity to encourage.

- When you share, you care!

CHAPTER 6: VICTORY

THE HIGHEST HONOR

THE HIGHEST HONOR

I first met Danny Fuhr when he was 9 years old. Danny was a little guy with a big idea: Danny knew he wanted to be great. Danny had bright eyes, and when Danny smiled, which was virtually all the time, his smile lit up the room. Danny was very respectful, highly coachable, and extremely focused for a young person. It was clear that he developed his work ethic from his family. Like many other multi-sport athletes, Danny came to Speed Track and Field to improve his speed. He was an exceptional football and baseball player. In fact Danny had once scored four touchdowns in one football game. Because of Danny's athletic prowess and involvement in multiple sports throughout the year, the only time I worked with him was during the winter season.

The Speed Track and Field practices were highly structured, highly organized, and offered scientific based training. The coaching staff was amazing and knew how to bring the best out of each individual despite their levels of ability and skill, and most flourished in this program if they applied themselves.

Danny was a decent sprinter. He had ventured into the long jump, and in 2012, he tried his efforts at the hurdles. This kid was athletic. I believe that Danny had a lot to do with bringing new athletes to the team. Because of his success in his non-track related sports as well as his blazing speed, Danny was, and continues to be, a walking endorsement for Speed Track and Field.

During one of our winter seasons, a few of Danny's baseball teammates were involved in our program. They were also good kids. For example, when Danny or his teammates were given instruction or constructive criticism, they would always refer to me as Coach or sir. Kids like Danny truly give me hope for the future of our youth. I recall giving Danny some feedback regarding his hurdle technique. I had been working with Danny for approximately three seasons and had become very familiar with his paraverbals. For example, whenever Danny was nervous or uncertain, he would rub the back of his neck. After we had talked, he walked away rubbing the back of his neck. I motioned for Danny to come back and told him that when he comes to practice, he must not check his hat at the door. "Danny you possess a stunning intellect. You are very intelligent; much smarter than I am. And that is a good thing. I want you to know that it is okay to question authority, just as long as you respect it." I continued, "Have I earned your respect?" He said that I had.

"In that case, feel free to ask me for clarification if you need to when I am giving you feedback. It is important that you are not at the mercy of any coach. I want you to learn how to think for yourself. If something doesn't make sense, ask for clarification." Danny immediately stopped rubbing the back of his neck. After that point, he felt empowered enough to ask questions at will.

Speed Track and Field had completed another season, and Danny had experienced success in the long jump, hurdles, and the 60 meter dash. At the end of each season, there is a gathering for athletes, parents and coaches known as the end of season celebration. They are celebrations with food, fun, and the opportunity to offer praise, and suggestions, and to present awards to those who had performed well during the season. The athletes are called up, and a few words are spoken about each. This is a great opportunity to motivate, educate, and inspire. When athletes do not receive enough recognition for their accomplishments, there was potential for parents or athletes to become frustrated. However, that particular year's celebration seemed to go off without a hitch. In fact, for me it was very special.

The parents had gotten together and put together a quilt. The quilt squares were fashioned with pictures of the athletes and coaches. I was exhausted on my way home from the event. As a coach, for me to address 50 athletes individually in such a short period of time was very emotionally taxing. Now that I am in my fifties, I recognize how every season, win or lose, takes a heavy toll.

When I arrived home, I had a voicemail from a parent of one of my athletes. She was irate over the feedback that I offered her son at the celebration.

This young man had demonstrated tremendous athletic prowess; however, his work ethic left much to be desired. He was lazy and did not know the difference between an excuse and a reason. He had underachieved horribly, and I do not applaud mediocrity. My message to him was simple: do not let your talent outweigh your ambition. No one is going to *let* you win in the real world.

The problem was that no one had ever addressed his work ethic and attitude, and he had not been held accountable by many of the previous authority figures in his life. When he showed up late to practice, he was not permitted to practice. When we did report card checks, there would always be a grade or two missing from his sheet. I had followed up with his teacher and found out he was not attending class regularly, and when he did show up, he was the class clown. His peers had warned him that when he signed up for Speed Track and Field, his behavior would not be acceptable. He often tried to push the envelope. However, I did not give in; I pushed back.

When I returned her call, I listened to her concerns about how I handled things. I expressed my thoughts to her, letting her know that yes, this young man had tremendous athletic prowess. However, if he was to become a productive member of society, he would have to parallel his athletic prowess with equal amounts of integrity and character. Based on my observations, he was not there yet. I thanked her for the opportunity to work with her son, and offered my best wishes for him in the future.

Conversely, the next day I received an email from Danny's parents. It was unbelievable. Danny's parents thanked us for another wonderful season and had a request of me. Danny wanted to know if I would baptize him. I was stunned and excited. This was the first time in my coaching life that I had received a request such as this. While I am not a pastor, I have never shied away from the fact that God is the center of my life. We would sometimes begin or end practice with a prayer. I would also periodically recite scripture or anecdotes from the Bible. But a baptism was different.

I called Danny's dad and let him know how grateful and honored I was by the request. He reiterated that this was Danny's idea, and as a family, they supported him. For clarification purposes, I asked him if he knew that I was not a pastor. He laughed and said that he knew. He added that I demonstrate the "saltiness" of someone who believes in the Lord. I believe that he may have been referring to the scripture found in Matthew 5:13-17 in which Jesus is teaching about salt and light. I thanked him for the opportunity and gave thanks to my higher power.

Later that morning, I called my brother, Promise Lee, who is the founder and senior pastor of Relevant Word Ministries in Colorado Springs. I explained the situation to him and asked for his thoughts. Promise told me to go for it, and so it was decided.

A local church offered a curriculum that helped the youth learn more about Christ and the importance of baptism. Danny spent the next several months learning and growing as a Christian, and of course playing football and baseball.

Danny was baptized and it was a great day. Alongside Danny's parents were several of Danny's friends, and my wife. I shared the honor of baptizing Danny.

During my 24 years of coaching, I have had a chance to be a part of many successes and have watched athletes achieve great things at both the amateur and professional levels. I never accept responsibility for the successes or failures of these athletes. However, I do take pride in their accomplishments and have a certain degree of satisfaction. **As a coach, taking part in the baptism of Danny Fuhr, is the greatest honor that I will experience.** Thanks to Danny, I have learned that as figures of authority we are always on audition. Danny has inspired me to become a better coach. For me to become a better coach, I will have to continue to grow as a person.

Danny, you are one of the most inspirational people in my life.

Coach Lee

Coaching Points:

- We are always on audition.

- Opportunity is everywhere.

- "With great authority comes great responsibility." - Francois-Marie Arouet

CHAPTER 7: LEADERSHIP
CONVERSATIONS WITH A FRIEND

Conversations with a Friend

Upon reflecting on some of the most influential people in my life, it would certainly be a mistake not to include Gene Southerland, also known as Mr. G. Mr. G is truly an icon in the city of Colorado Springs. He is the consummate business professional. People from all walks of life come to his place of business. Once you have spoken with Mr. G. it is apparent that he possesses a stunning intellect. Over the years, he has provided me with a roadmap of sorts on how to handle the ebb and flow of life.

M&M's®, Snickers®, and Bit-O-Honey®

As a kid, perhaps around 9 or 10 years old, I remember being at Mr. G's listening to the older people talk. The only thing that distracted me from listening was the jar that was placed on his desk. Mr. G had a jar full of M&M's, Snickers, and of course, Bit-O-Honey, which were my absolute favorite. I never, ever had a chance to enjoy one of those candy bars like some of the other kids did because the candy was for sale, but it did not stop me from looking at them. Like I said earlier, Mr. G was a business professional. Though he was, and still tends to be, very philanthropic, he did not give many things away. Even back then, Mr. G was teaching me something essential about business. The lesson was a simple one: **business is business.**

THE TEACHER

Mr. G was gifted at making every customer feel like royalty. Upon entering his business, you felt like you were in a sanctuary. Mr. G was a teacher without a blackboard or lesson plan. His lesson was hidden in plain sight: **treat everyone with dignity and respect.**

THE COACH

The years between 1998 and 2002 were incredibly difficult for me. I was challenged on many fronts. The death of my son, premature birth of my daughter, divorce, and loss of my job had all taken their respective tolls. I was a fraction of myself. I had no self-esteem. In fact, I had developed a sense of shame. I was embarrassed with where my life was, and it was apparent to those who knew me and cared that I simply was not myself. Searching for answers, I went to see Mr. G to discuss my situation with him. Mr. G was sympathetic to my state; however, he had no tolerance for my "poor me" attitude.

His instruction was simple. Don't forget who you are. You are not the sum total of your circumstances.

He offered me a fresh perspective telling me that I had weathered the storm and that I was courageous. He then asked me what was next. He was calling me a champion without doing so. He was motivating me in a counterintuitive way. He was reminding me that quitting was not an option. There was nothing I could do to change the past; however, if I could recognize the strength I had gained as a person who had endured such a series of struggles, there was no mountain I could not conquer.

THE RELATIONSHIP

Mr. G and I discussed many things; however, one of our favorite topics of discussions was the sport of track and field. He was a sports enthusiast, and the fact that I was a track coach made this topic very interesting to both of us. I recall sharing the story about some of the challenges that a local middle school, where I coached, was experiencing. The administration and the teachers were at odds, and it was creating some issues in the school. Moral had slipped to an all-time low. Some of the teachers had resigned or quit, and the students were suffering the repercussions. Athletically, the school had not won a girls' track and field championship in 73 years. I believed that if our efforts on the track resulted in a championship, the school would gain some traction on the downward spiral on which it was heading. Mr. G and I discussed this, and he encouraged me to go for it.

In 2011, the North Middle School girls' track and field team beat their rivals and won the Colorado Springs Classic title. That evening, the administrators, teachers, parents, and student athletes celebrated the victory. The competition was also aired on a local television station and reinforced the value of continued hard work and cooperation. At our next meeting, I shared the outcome with Mr. G and he applauded the effort.

Mr. G and I reconnected in the summer of 2012 and had a chance to share our thoughts on the 2012 Olympic Games. Of course, there were several highlights; however, for us, there was nothing greater than watching four of the fastest female sprinters in the United States execute a picture-perfect baton exchange, resulting in a new world record in the 4x100 meter relay.

Lessons from the Heart

On another occasion I remember sharing a conversation with Mr. G about a phone conversation I had with my father-in-law. Over the last several years, my wife's mother had developed a severe case of depression. The disease was extremely debilitating, rendering her helpless in many aspects of her life. We had been on the phone with her family one morning, and I inquired on how Mom was doing. I always felt like I was part of my wife's family. In fact, I even called her mother "Mom". My wife's father Gerald told me that mom was having a tough day. Due to the depression, she had developed an uncontrollable shaking of her hands and was not able to tie her shoes. I recall commenting that it must be tough for him, but before I could finish my thought, he replied, "Charmas, I thank God for the opportunity to tie Patricia's shoes."

I have to tell you that his comment riveted me. I learned through our exchange that there was another level of care for someone you love. What I had interpreted as a burden, he saw as a blessing.

Scripture says, "Husbands, love your wives like Christ loved the church."

That passage made more sense at that moment than ever before. That conversation completely changed the nature of my relationship with my wife.

A LIVING TESTIMONY

As I stated at the beginning of this chapter, Mr. G has provided me with a roadmap to life and how to cope with its inevitable ups and downs. Mr. G gives great advice. He also practices what he preaches. Over the last couple of years I had noticed that Mr. G's wife Rita was sometimes in the shop. I was there every three to four weeks, and Rita was there every time I was. Mr. G would bring Rita to work with him, where she would remain the entire day. While she was there Mr. G attended to her every need. Things had changed. Rita was no longer herself. Concerned, I inquired and was told that she was struggling with dementia.

I went out of town for a couple of weeks, and when I returned for an appointment with Mr. G, Rita was not there. I did not have to ask—I knew she had gone on to meet the Lord. Mr. G had reinforced a valuable lesson. The lesson was about commitment. He had committed to love his wife to her final day.

The education that I received from Mr. G helped shape my business model. He taught me how important it was to be a professional. He stressed that anything worth doing is worth doing right. He taught me to be community-minded, but to also be sure to take care of business. Mr. G knew I had a big heart; he also knew that if I was not careful with regard to business, I would give too much away. Most importantly, he inspired me through his actions and the way he took care of Rita during challenging times.

So, who is Mr. G? Was he a psychologist, teacher, accountant, or perhaps even a preacher? No. The valuable lessons I learned from Mr. G came in 30 to 45 minutes increments while I sat in his barber's chair. This magnificent man, full of encouragement and wisdom, is my barber. It is funny how life's most important things are often hidden in plain sight. If we are willing to pay attention, take instruction, and follow through, we may come to recognize the most valuable things in life are all around us.

Mr. G, thank you for all you have done to help shape me into the man I am today. Blessings, my friend!

Charmas Lee

Coaching Points:

- Treat everyone with dignity and respect.

- Possess the mind of a king, the heart of a servant, and the work ethic of a warrior.

- Love your spouse with all your heart, soul, and mind.

CHAPTER 8: LOVE

LIFE SAVERS

Life Savers

This is a short story—a brief insight—on the most positive motivating force within my life (with the exception of my higher power): Mrs. Janice Lee.

"Down goes Frazier," shouts Howard Cosell during the second round of the much anticipated Heavyweight Championship fight between George Foreman and Joe Frazier.

"Down goes Frazier," Cosell exclaims a second time with a high sense of urgency, concern, disbelief and desperation as if though he was hoping that the referee was listening and ready to step in and stop the fight.

Frazier got to his feet only to be knocked down again and again, eventually leading to the fight being scored a technical knockout. The referee stepped in and stopped the onslaught. His decision to stop the fight probably saved Joe Frazier's life. George Foreman was too big, fast, and strong.

Life had become the George Foreman of my current existence. I was Joe Frazier, and was not able to get back on my feet. The ambush was on, and I desperately needed the referee to step in. I was in a funk, a downward spiral, perhaps even a state of sorrow that left me absent. Defeated by life, I began to seriously consider an exit strategy.

A 42 year old man, who had lost his sense of self, a failure at least by the world's terms. Unimportant and worthless, nobody cared; at least this was the doom-loop that played over and over in my head. Life had hit me with a series of sucker punches that left me unresponsive. On this day I was on life's canvas floor and didn't plan on attempting to get back up. As I contemplated my exit strategy a car pulled into the parking lot. It was a former client, a nice lady with a great smile. I asked her if she had a moment, she looked at her watch and said yes.

I summed up the courage to share what was happening in my life, communicated the pain that I was experiencing and my feelings of worthlessness. Embarrassed, I thanked her for listening and shook my head as I walked away. Articulating my situation had heightened my sense of reality, and all glimmers of hope had taken a back seat to despair. The lyrics of an old Temptations song became an interloper in my head "...*The sun is shining, there's plenty of light, a new day's dawning sunny and bright, but after I've been crying all night, the sun is cold and the new day seems old. Determination is fading fast; inspiration is a thing of the past. Can't see how my hopes gonna last, good things are bad and what was happy is sad."*

That was it; that was the knockout punch. My internal referee proclaimed, "Down goes Charmas, down goes Charmas!" Suddenly, I heard a voice from the heavens; I heard the voice of an angel.

"Charmas, don't sell yourself short."

"Don't sell yourself short," were the most encouraging words that I had heard in a long time. I interpreted it as a message of hope, a light in the dark, a short break from the silent pain that I was experiencing. Maybe I still had value. Maybe this was my lifeline; I had something to cling to.

I took a deep breath, followed by a brief sigh of relief. I felt like I had been snatched from the gallows and been given a reprieve on life. Slightly energized with hope, I went back to work at the fitness and sports center. Encouraged, I began to work with my clients until lunchtime, when Janice came into the facility. When she asked how I was doing, my heart leapt. Her voice was music to my ears; there was something about the voice. I sensed a sincere concern in her voice; it was a question from the heart. I told her that I was doing fine. And for the moment, I *was* fine. It is amazing the power that words can carry. They can humor, soothe, hurt, or heal. On this particular occasion, those words were a source of inspiration. I was not out of the woods yet. Each day brought with it its own set of challenges. Because of the stress and uncertainty of life at the time, it became more difficult to stay upbeat.

Janice's smile brought light into the dark place where I was currently living. I believed that she must be a modern day angel that walked the earth sent from the heavens for a time such as this.

Over a short period of time, Janice and I got to know each other better. We became friends and eventually we began to date. I fell in love with her. Uncertain of how to convey the nature of my feelings, I summoned up the courage to be completely transparent with her, sharing my strengths and weaknesses and previous derailments from my path in life. I had a very uncertain future; however, what I shared with her was that I loved her and I knew that God had a plan for me. I just did not know what it was.

After bearing my soul to her, I figured she would dismiss me and my feelings. Much to my surprise, she communicated her love for me as well. Janice and I were married in 2003, and with her by my side, sometimes leading sometimes following, she has helped me accomplish things *greater than I could have ever imagined.*

In 2007 Janice resigned from her position as the Assistant Human Resources Officer at the United States Air Force Academy. Today, she is my business partner and the president of two highly successful businesses that promote positive change in other's lives. She also continues to be the positive motivating force in my life.

Janice you have inspired me in many ways....Thank you for being my coach!

Charmas Lee

Coaching Points:

- You are never as alone as you feel.

- Joy may be one thought or spoken word away.

- We are all human lifesavers.

My Lifetime Value

I have learned that one's best may be achieved in both victory and defeat...I recognize that my lifetime value cannot be measured by a dollar amount or simply in a win-loss column. Once the dust clears and it's all said and done, my legacy will be determined by the words I have left behind that were grounded in truth and will be determined by the number of lives that I have changed for the better.

Actions Steps

Pause, reflect and take some time to consider the stories that you have read. Each story was inspired by true events. There is also a story within each story, a subtle message that if recognized and applied can change your trajectory in life.

I encourage you to develop a statement of significance which will give rise to your voice and help keep you focused in the turbulent times. The statement of significance contains three points: (1) The value of your life experiences (2) A brief synopsis of what you have learned and (3) Armed with knowledge of self and a fresh perspective, communicate the positive impact you will make on the rest of the world.

Below you will find my personal statements of significance, purpose and mission.

STATEMENT OF SIGNIFICANCE

I choose to recognize the value of every life experience, knowing that each one has helped me become the person that I am today. Life is a continuous process of education. Because of this knowledge, I promise to work in a spirit of cooperation with others to create a positive learning environment modeling a shining example for all. I commit to serving mankind faithfully, using my personal experiences, my life story, to encourage, motivate, direct, educate and influence others to develop a sense of greater expectations within themselves. There is nothing wrong with hard work. Sweat equity builds character and good character is the foundation of all that will ever be achieved. I recognize that because of my ability to influence others, it is imperative that I am honest, straightforward, trustworthy, consistent, transparent, authentic and sincere. I know that I am always on audition.

STATEMENT OF PURPOSE

Create a positive change in the lives of others.

STATEMENT OF MISSION

Motivate, educate and inspire others to develop a sense of greater expectations within themselves.

Appendix

Charmas' Guiding Principles for Daily Living

1. Treat everyone with dignity and respect.

2. Don't major in minor things.

3. Commit to constant self-improvement.

4. Be modest.

5. Expect the extraordinary.

6. Maintain a high standard of excellence for yourself and others.

7. Help others grow mentally, physically, spiritually, athletically and academically.

8. Continuously condition the mind for success.

9. Recognize defining moments and give thanks.

10. Be brave, bold and say thank you every time you get the chance.

ABOUT THE AUTHOR

Charmas Lee is a husband, father, highly successful coach, and the owner of three businesses located in Colorado Springs, Colorado, that specialize in human performance: Building Champions, a business that offers professional development through personal empowerment; Building Better Bodies, a sports performance business that offers top-shelf training to those who desire to compete at optimal levels of sport; and Speed T&F (of which he is also the founder and Executive Director), a national-caliber USA Track and Field Junior Olympic youth athletic educational program. Mr. Lee is a sport and fitness professional certified through the American College of Sports Medicine and the National Strength and Conditioning Association. He is also one of few Certified Level 3 USA Track and Field coaches qualified to coach athletes at the Olympic level. He is the former physical conditioning specialist at the USAFA Preparatory School. Mr. Lee plays a significant role in the development of various amateur and professional athletes across the country.

For further information about Charmas B. Lee, his articles, upcoming books and schedule of presentations and public talks go to www.charmaslee.com.

Charmas B. Lee
Building Champions
Author-Speaker-Motivator
Certified Strength and Conditioning Specialist, NSCA
Certified Health and Fitness Specialist, ACSM
Level 3 Track and Field Coach, USATF
Level 2 Coach Sprints, Hurdles, Relays and Endurance, USATF

Made in the USA
Charleston, SC
12 March 2013